50 RUSSIAN FOLK SONGS

arranged and edited by

PETER I. TSCHAIKOVSKY

CD 3042

MMO CD 3042

TSCHAIKOVSKY
50 RUSSIAN FOLK SONGS
For Piano Four Hands

✱**Note:** The final two selections can be found on program 99. This is due to the fact that CD players do not go above a 99 song selection.

4

Secondo
1. The Young Girl

3 taps + 1 precede music.

Andante non troppo.

2. Chimes

2 taps precede music.

Moderato.

1. The Young Girl

2. Chimes

Secondo
3. Remember, My Dear

4 taps precede music.

Andante.

4. The Waves

3 taps precede music.

Tranquillo.

3. Remember, My Dear

4 taps precede music.

Andante.

4. The Waves

3 taps precede music.

Tranquillo.

8

5. Do Not Overflow, My Quiet Don

Primo
5. Do Not Overflow, My Quiet Don

10

6. Spin, My Spinning Wheel

7. The New House

6. Spin, My Spinning Wheel

7. The New House

12

8. Awakening

Moderato.   3 taps precede music.

9. Faded Flowers

Moderato.   3 taps precede music.

Primo
8. Awakening

9. Faded Flowers

Secondo

Secondo
10. Floating

2 taps precede music.
Allegro moderato.

11. My Green Grapes

4 taps (2 measures) precede music.
Allegro.

Primo
10. Floating

11. My Green Grapes

4 taps (2 measures) precede music.

Secondo
12. Howl Not, Strong Winds

13. Twilight

12. Howl Not, Strong Winds

Andante.   2 taps precede music.

4 taps (2 measures) precede music.

13. Twilight

Allegro vivo.

Secondo

14. With Bowed Head

15. Sunrise

14. With Bowed Head

15. Sunrise

Secondo
16. Sing Not, Oh, Lark

Moderato.   3 taps precede music.

17. Andrei Goes For A Walk

Allegro risoluto.   4 taps (2 measures) precede music.

16. Sing Not, Oh, Lark

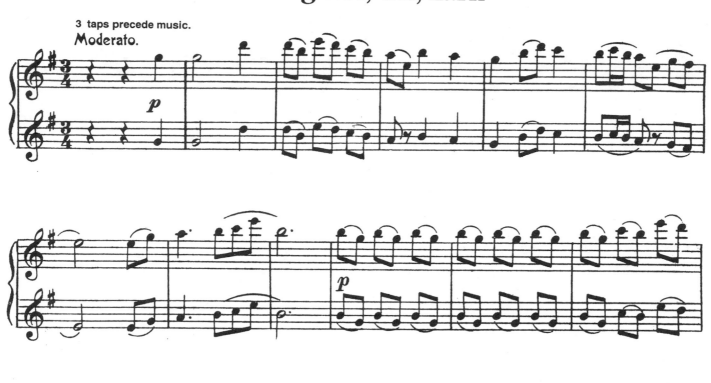

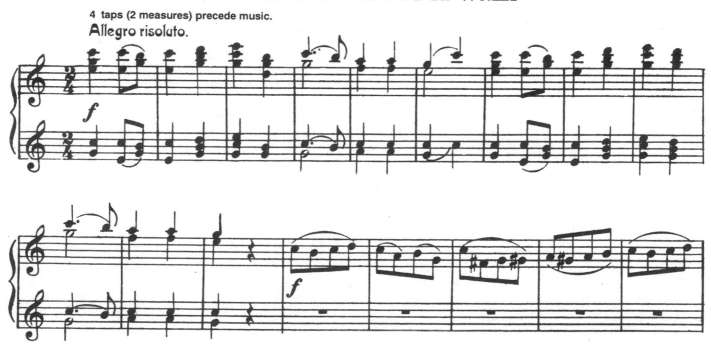

17. Andrei Goes For A Walk

Secondo

Secondo
18. The Little Duck

Moderato con moto. 2 taps precede music.

Primo
18. The Little Duck

Secondo
19. Festival

Moderato.   2 taps precede music.

20. I Shall Come To Your City

Allegro moderato.   4 taps (2 measures) precede music.

19. Festival

20. I Shall Come To Your City

30

Secondo
21. My Heart Yearns

2 taps (2/3 meas.) precede music.

Andante mosso.

22. From The Mountains

3 taps (1½ meas.) precede music.

Andante.

Primo
21. My Heart Yearns

2 taps (2/3 meas.) precede music.

Andante mosso.

22. From The Mountains

3 taps (1½ meas.) precede music.

Andante.

Secondo

23. The Duck Swims On The Sea

24. The Three-Cornered Handkerchief

Primo
23. The Duck Swims On The Sea

24. The Three-Cornered Handkerchief

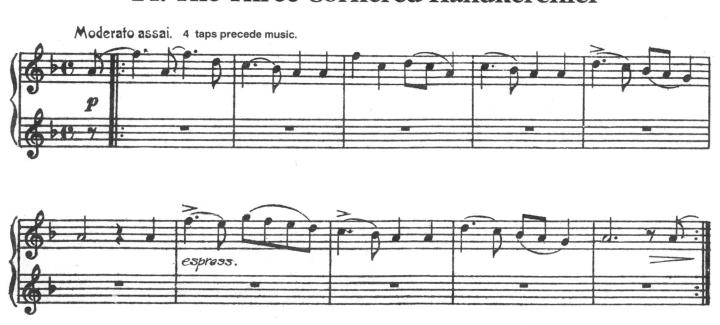

Secondo
25. The Green Meadow Behind Our Yard

26. The Farm

25. The Green Meadow Behind Our Yard

26. The Farm

Secondo
27. The Blue Sea

3 taps precede music.
Moderato.

28. Along The Green Meadow

Andante. 2 taps precede music.

Primo
27. The Blue Sea

28. Along The Green Meadow

Secondo

29. Wine Feast

Moderato. 2 taps precede music.

29. Wine Feast

Moderato.   2 taps precede music.

Secondo
30. Approaching The City

Moderato. 2 taps precede music.

31. The Abbot

Moderato. 3 taps precede music.

Primo
30. Approaching The City

31. The Abbot

42

Secondo
32. Dance

Allegro non troppo. 2 taps precede music.

Primo
32. Dance

44

33. In The Green Fields

34. My Gay Katya

Primo
33. In The Green Fields

34. My Gay Katya

Secondo
35. Oh, My Poor Heart!

36. My Little Duck

Primo
35. Oh, My Poor Heart!

36. My Little Duck

Secondo
37. The Little Girl

3 taps precede music.

Allegro moderato.

38. Play, My Guitar!

3 taps precede music.

Allegro.

Primo

37. The Little Girl

3 taps precede music.

Allegro moderato.

38. Play, My Guitar!

3 taps precede music.

Allegro.

Secondo
39. Oh, My Fields, My Fields

2 taps precede music.

Andante non troppo.

40. The Square Dance

3 taps precede music.

Andante.

marcato con espr.

Primo
39. Oh, My Fields, My Fields

2 taps precede music.
Andante non troppo.

40. The Square Dance

3 taps precede music.
Andante.

Secondo
41. The Rooster

4 taps precede music.

42. Under The Green Apple Tree

2 taps precede music.

Primo
41. The Rooster

42. Under The Green Apple Tree

Secondo
43. My Fields

44. The Queen

Primo
43. My Fields

Andante. 2 taps precede music.

44. The Queen

2 taps precede music.
Moderato.

Secondo
45. Picking Berries

Andante. 2 taps precede music.

46. Meadows

Andante non troppo. 2 taps precede music.

Primo
45. Picking Berries

Andante. 2 taps precede music.

46. Meadows

Allegro non troppo. 2 taps precede music.

Secondo
47. Vanya

48. At The Gate

Primo
47. Vanya

48. At The Gate

60

49. Song Of The Volga Boatmen

50. Tranquilllity

49. Song Of The Volga Boatmen

Moderato. 2 taps precede music.

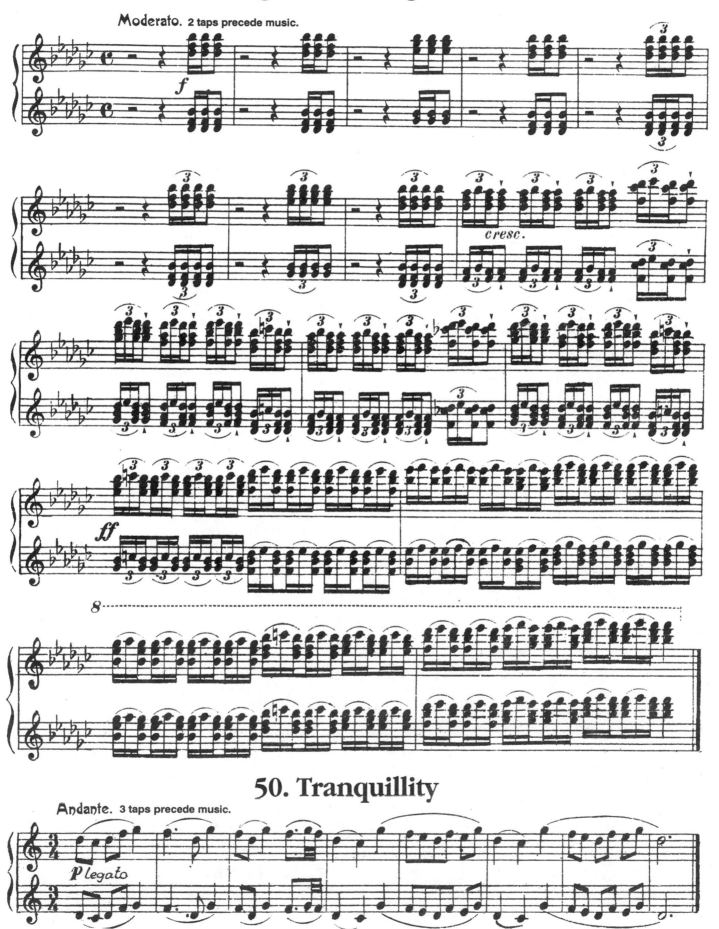

50. Tranquillity

Andante. 3 taps precede music.

Music Minus One POPULAR MUSIC Compact Discs

- __ MMO CD 1001 Hits Of Frank Sinatra
- __ MMO CD 1002 Hits Of Barbara Streisand
- __ MMO CD 1004 Hits Of Elvis Presley
- __ MMO CD 1005 Hits Of The Beatles
- __ MMO CD 1008 Hits Of Roy Orbison
- __ MMO CD 1009 Hits Of Patsy Cline
- __ MMO CD 1011 Hits Of Billy Joel
- __ MMO CD 1012 Hits Of Linda Ronstadt
- __ MMO CD 1013 Hits Of The Carpenters
- __ MMO CD 1017 Hits Of Ray Charles
- __ MMO CD 1019 Hits Of Anita Baker
- __ MMO CD 1020 Hits Of Sammy Davis Jr./Anthony Newley
- __ MMO CD 1024 George Gershwin Favorites
- __ MMO CD 1025 Songs Of Cole Porter
- __ MMO CD 1027 Hits Of Diana Ross
- __ MMO CD 1028 Hits Of Tom Jones
- __ MMO CD 1029 Hits Of Bobby Darin & Frank Sinatra
- __ MMO CD 1032 Hits Of Nat "King" Cole
- __ MMO CD 1066 Hits Of Rock And Roll
- __ MMO CDG 101 Hits Of Patsy Cline
- __ MMO CDG 102 Country Female Hits
- __ MMO CDG 103 Country Male Hits
- __ MMO CDG 104 Country Male Classics
- __ MMO CDG 105 Great Standards
- __ MMO CDG 106 Pop Male Hits
- __ MMO CDG 107 Pop Female Hits
- __ MMO CDG 108 Great Love Songs
- __ MMO CDG 109 Hits Of The 60's
- __ MMO CDG 110 Hits Of The 50's
- __ MMO CDG 111 Children's Favorites
- __ MMO CDG 112 Christmas Favorites
- __ MMO CDG 113 Hits Of Neil Diamond, vol. 1
- __ MMO CDG 114 Hits Of The Carpenters
- __ MMO CDG 115 Hits Of Elton John
- __ MMO CDG 116 Hits Of Barbara Streisand
- __ MMO CDG 117 Hits Of Frank Sinatra
- __ MMO CDG 118 Hits Of Elvis Presley
- __ MMO CDG 119 Greatest Sing-Alongs
- __ MMO CDG 120 Hits Of Bette Midler
- __ MMO CDG 121 Best Of Broadway
- __ MMO CDG 122 Hits Of Whitney Houston
- __ MMO CDG 123 Hits Of Linda Ronstadt
- __ MMO CDG 124 Old Tyme Sing-Alongs
- __ MMO CDG 125 Hits Of Neil Diamond, vol. 2
- __ MMO CDG 126 Happy Songs Are Here Again
- __ MMO CDG 127 The Coasters & The Drifters
- __ MMO CDG 128 Love Songs For A Wedding
- __ MMO CDG 132 Female Chart Toppers
- __ MMO CDG 135 Country Females
- __ MMO CDG 137 Hits Of Neil Diamond, vol. 3
- __ MMO CDG 139 The Platters

Music Minus One PIANO Compact Discs

- __ MMO CD 3001 Beethoven Piano Concerto No. 1 in C, Opus 15
- __ MMO CD 3002 Beethoven Piano Concerto No. 2 in Bb, Opus 19
- __ MMO CD 3003 Beethoven Piano Concerto No. 3 in Cm, Opus 37
- __ MMO CD 3004 Beethoven Piano Concerto No. 4 in G, Opus 58
- __ MMO CD 3005 Beethoven Piano Concerto No. 5 in Eb, Opus 73   2 CD Set
- __ MMO CD 3006 Grieg Piano Concerto in A minor, Opus 16
- __ MMO CD 3007 Rachmaninoff Piano Concerto No. 2 in C minor
- __ MMO CD 3008 Schumann Piano Concerto in A minor, Opus 54
- __ MMO CD 3009 Brahms Piano Concerto No. 1 in D minor, Opus 15, 2 CD Set
- __ MMO CD 3010 Chopin Piano Concerto No. 1 in Em, Opus 11
- __ MMO CD 3011 Mendelssohn Piano Concerto No. 1 in Gm, Opus 25
- __ MMO CD 3012 W.A. Mozart Piano Concerto No. 9 in Ebm, K.271
- __ MMO CD 3013 W.A. Mozart Piano Concerto No. 12 in A, K.414
- __ MMO CD 3014 W.A. Mozart Piano Concerto No. 20 in Dm, K.466
- __ MMO CD 3015 W.A. Mozart Piano Concerto No. 23 in A, K.488
- __ MMO CD 3016 W.A. Mozart Piano Concerto No. 24 in Cm, K.491
- __ MMO CD 3017 W.A. Mozart Piano Concerto No. 26 in D, 'Coronation'
- __ MMO CD 3018 W.A. Mozart Piano Concerto in G major, K.453
- __ MMO CD 3019 Liszt Piano Concerto No. 1/Weber Concertstucke
- __ MMO CD 3020 Liszt Piano Concerto No. 2/Hungarian Fantasia
- __ MMO CD 3021 J.S. Bach Piano Concerto in Fm/J.C. Bach Concerto in Eb
- __ MMO CD 3022 J.S. Bach Piano Concerto in D minor
- __ MMO CD 3023 Haydn Piano Concerto in D major
- __ MMO CD 3024 Heart Of The Piano Concerto
- __ MMO CD 3025 Themes From The Great Piano Concerti
- __ MMO CD 3026 Tschiakowsky Piano Concerto No. 1 in Bbm, Opus 23
- __ MMO CD 3027 Rachmaninoff: Six Scenes for 4 Hands
- __ MMO CD 3028 Arensky: Six Pieces
    Stravinsky: 3 Dances: March/Valse/Polka
- __ MMO CD 3029 Faure: Dolly Suite - 4 hands
- __ MMO CD 3031 Schumann: Pictures from the East
    6 Impromtus for 4 hands
- __ MMO CD 3032 Beethoven: Three Marches, Op. 45 4 hands

Music Minus One VOCALIST Compact Discs

- __ MMO CD 4001 Schubert Lieder for High Voice
- __ MMO CD 4002 Schubert Lieder for Low Voice
- __ MMO CD 4003 Schubert Lieder for High Voice volume 2
- __ MMO CD 4004 Schubert Lieder for Low Voice volume 2
- __ MMO CD 4005 Brahms Lieder for High Voice
- __ MMO CD 4006 Brahms Lieder for Low Voice
- __ MMO CD 4007 Everybody's Favorite Songs for High Voice
- __ MMO CD 4008 Everybody's Favorite Songs for Low Voice
- __ MMO CD 4009 Everybody's Favorite Songs for High Voice volume 2
- __ MMO CD 4010 Everybody's Favorite Songs for Low Voice volume 2
- __ MMO CD 4011 17th/18th Century Italian Songs High Voice
- __ MMO CD 4012 17th/18th Century Italian Songs Low Voice
- __ MMO CD 4013 17th/18th Century Italian Songs High Voice volume 2
- __ MMO CD 4014 17th/18th Century Italian Songs Low Voice volume 2
- __ MMO CD 4015 Famous Soprano Arias
- __ MMO CD 4016 Famous Mezzo-Soprano Arias
- __ MMO CD 4017 Famous Tenor Arias
- __ MMO CD 4018 Famous Baritone Arias
- __ MMO CD 4019 Famous Bass Arias
- __ MMO CD 4020 Hugo Wolf Lieder for High Voice
- __ MMO CD 4021 Hugo Wolf Lieder for Low Voice
- __ MMO CD 4022 Richard Strauss Lieder for High Voice
- __ MMO CD 4023 Richard Strauss Lieder for Low Voice
- __ MMO CD 4024 Robert Schumann Lieder for High Voice
- __ MMO CD 4025 Robert Schumann Lieder for Low Voice
- __ MMO CD 4026 W.A. Mozart Arias For Soprano
- __ MMO CD 4027 Verdi Arias For Soprano
- __ MMO CD 4028 Italian Arias For Soprano
- __ MMO CD 4029 French Arias For Soprano
- __ MMO CD 4030 Soprano Oratorio Arias
- __ MMO CD 4031 Alto Oratorio Arias
- __ MMO CD 4032 Tenor Oratorio Arias
- __ MMO CD 4033 Bass Oratorio Arias

Choice selections for the Vocalist, drawn from the very best solo literature for the voice. Professional artists perform these pieces to guide the singer in interpreting each piece.

- * MMO CD 4041 Beginning Soprano Solos   Kate Hurney, soprano
- * MMO CD 4042 Intermediate Soprano Solos   Kate Hurney, soprano
- * MMO CD 4043 Beginning Mezzo Sop. Solos   Fay Kittleson, mezzo-sop.
- * MMO CD 4044 Intermediate Mezzo-Sop. Solos Fay Kittleson, mezzo-sop.
- * MMO CD 4045 Advanced Mezzo-Sop. Solos   Fay Kittleson, mezzo-sop.
- * MMO CD 4046 Beginning Contralto Solos   Carline Ray, mezzo-sop.
- * MMO CD 4047 Beginning Tenor Solos   George Shirley, tenor
- * MMO CD 4048 Intermediate Tenor Solos   George Shirley, tenor
- * MMO CD 4049 Advance Tenor Solos   George Shirley, tenor

* Winter '95/Spring '96 Release

Music Minus One VIOLIN Compact Discs

- __ MMO CD 3100 Bruch Violin Concerto in Gm
- __ MMO CD 3101 Mendelssohn Violin Concerto in Em
- __ MMO CD 3102 Tschaikovsky Violin Concerto in D, Opus 35
- __ MMO CD 3103 J.S. Bach "Double" Concerto in Dm
- __ MMO CD 3104 J.S. Bach Violin Concerti in Am/E
- __ MMO CD 3105 J.S. Bach Brandenburg Concerti Nos. 4 and 5
- __ MMO CD 3106 J.S. Bach Brandenburg No. 2/Triple Concerto
- __ MMO CD 3107 J.S. Bach Concerto in Dm
- __ MMO CD 3108 Brahms Violin Concerto in D, Opus 77
- __ MMO CD 3109 Chausson Poeme/Schubert Rondo
- __ MMO CD 3110 Lalo Symphonie Espagnole
- __ MMO CD 3111 Mozart Concerto in D/Vivaldi Concerto in Am
- __ MMO CD 3112 Mozart Violin Concerto in A, K.219
- __ MMO CD 3113 Wieniawski Concerto in D/Sarasate Zigeunerweisen
- __ MMO CD 3114 Viotto Concerto No. 22
- __ MMO CD 3115 Beethoven Two Romances/"Spring" Sonata
- __ MMO CD 3116 St. Saëns Intro & Rondo Cap./Mozart Serenade & Adagio
- __ MMO CD 3117 Beethoven Violin Concerto in D major, Opus 61, 2 CD Set
- __ MMO CD 3118 The Concertmaster Solos from Symphonic Works
- __ MMO CD 3119 Air On A G String Favorite Encores for Orchestra
- __ MMO CD 3120 Concert Pieces For The Serious Violinist
- __ MMO CD 3121 Eighteenth Century Violin Music
- __ MMO CD 3122 Violin Favorites With Orchestra Vol. 1 (Easy)
- __ MMO CD 3123 Violin Favorites With Orchestra Vol. 2 (Moderate)
- __ MMO CD 3124 Violin Favorites With Orchestra Vol. 3 (Mod. Diff.)
- __ MMO CD 3125 The Three B's: Bach/Beethoven/Brahms
- __ MMO CD 3126 Vivaldi Concerti in Am, D, Am Opus 3 No. 6,9,8
- __ MMO CD 3127 Vivaldi "The Four Seasons" 2 CD set $29.98 each
- __ MMO CD 3128 Vivaldi "La Tempesta di Mare" Opus 8 No. 5
    Albinoni: Violin Concerto in A
- __ MMO CD 3129 Vivaldi: Violin Concerto Opus 3 No. 12
    Vivaldi Violin Concerto Opus 8, No. 6 "Il Piacere"
- __ MMO CD 3130 Schubert Three Sonatina, Opus 137
- __ MMO CD 3131 Haydn String Quartet No. 1 in G, Op. 76
- __ MMO CD 3132 Haydn String Quartet No. 2 in d, Op. 76
- __ MMO CD 3133 Haydn String Quartet No. 3 in C, Op. 76 "Emperor"
- __ MMO CD 3134 Haydn String Quartet No. 4 in Bb, Op. 76 "Sunrise"
- __ MMO CD 3135 Haydn String Quartet No. 5 in D, Op. 76
- __ MMO CD 3136 Haydn String Quartet No. 6 in Eb, Op. 76

Music Minus One CELLO Compact Discs

___ MMO CD 3701 Dvorak: Cello Concerto in B minor, Opus 104
___ MMO CD 3702 C.P.E. Bach: Cello Concerto in A minor
___ MMO CD 3703 Boccherini: Concerto in Bb Major; Bruch: Kol Nidrei

Music Minus One GUITAR Compact Discs

___ MMO CD 3601 Boccherini: Guitar Quintet, No. 4 in D major
___ MMO CD 3602 Giuliani: Guitar Quintet, Opus 65
___ MMO CD 3603 Classic Guitar Duets Easy - Medium
___ MMO CD 3604 Renaissance & Baroque Guitar Duets
___ MMO CD 3605 Classical & Romantic Guitar Duets
___ MMO CD 3606 Guitar & Flute Duets, vol. 1
___ MMO CD 3607 Play The Folk Guitar, Dick Weissman/Dan Fox
___ MMO CD 3608 Play The Guitar (Single String), Gene Leis
___ MMO CD 3609 Play The Guitar 'Pop' Method, George Barnes

Music Minus One FLUTE Compact Discs

___ MMO CD 3300 Mozart Concerto in D/Quantz Concerto in G
___ MMO CD 3301 Mozart Flute Concerto in G major
___ MMO CD 3302 J.S. Bach Suite No. 2 in Bm
___ MMO CD 3303 Boccherini/Vivaldi Concerti/Mozart Andante
___ MMO CD 3304 Haydn/Vivaldi/Frederick "The Great" Concerti
___ MMO CD 3305 Vivaldi/Telemann/Leclair Flute Concerti
___ MMO CD 3306 J.S. Bach Brandenburg No. 2/Haydn Concerto
___ MMO CD 3307 J.S. Bach Triple Concerto/Vivaldi Concerto No. 9
___ MMO CD 3308 Mozart/Stamitz Flute Quartets
___ MMO CD 3309 Haydn London Trios
___ MMO CD 3310 J.S. Bach Brandenburg Concerti No. 4 and No. 5
___ MMO CD 3311 W.A. Mozart Three Flute Quartets
___ MMO CD 3312 Telemann Am Suite/Gluck 'Orpheus' Scene/Pergolesi Conc. in G
___ MMO CD 3313 Flute Song Easy Familiar Classics
___ MMO CD 3314 Vivaldi 3 Flute Concerti RV 427, 438, Opus 10 No. 5
___ MMO CD 3315 Vivaldi 3 Flute Concerti RV 440, Opus 10 No. 4, RV 429
___ MMO CD 3316 Easy Solos, Student Editions, Beginning Level vol. 1
___ MMO CD 3317 Easy Solos, Student Editions, Beginning Level vol. 2
___ MMO CD 3318 Easy Jazz Duets, Student Editions, 1-3 years
___ MMO CD 3319 Flute & Guitar Duets, vol. 1
___ MMO CD 3320 Flute & Guitar Duets, vol. 2
___ MMO CD 3333 First Chair Flute Solos With Orchestra

Choice selections for the Flute, drawn from the very best solo literature for the instrument. The pieces are performed by the foremost virtuosi of our time, artists affiliated with the New York Philharmonic, Boston, Chicago, Cleveland and Philadelphia Orchestras. The Julliard School, Curtis Institute of Music, Indiana University, University of Toronto and Metropolitan Opera Orchestra.

Beginning	Intermediate	Advanced	Level
___ MMO CD 3321	Murray Panitz, Philadelphia Orch.		B
___ MMO CD 3322	Donald Peck, Chicago Symphony		B
___ MMO CD 3323	Julius Baker, N.Y. Philharmonic		I
___ MMO CD 3324	Donald Peck, Chicago Symphony		I
___ MMO CD 3325	Murray Panitz, Philadelphia Orch.		A
___ MMO CD 3326	Julius Baker, N.Y. Philharmonic		A
___ MMO CD 3327	Donald Peck, Chicago Symphony		I A
___ MMO CD 3328	Murray Panitz, Philadelphia Orch.		I A
___ MMO CD 3329	Julius Baker, N.Y. Philharmonic		I
___ MMO CD 3330	Doriot Dwyer, Boston Symphony		B
___ MMO CD 3331	Doriot Dwyer, Boston Symphony		I
___ MMO CD 3332	Doriot Dwyer, Boston Symphony		A

The repertoire and editions used in the Laureate Series correspond to the approved music lists of various Music Education Associations and may be performed as contest solos in State Music Festivals. Contest regulations, such as time limitations have been taken into consideration.

Music Minus One FRENCH HORN Compact Discs

___ MMO CD 3501 Mozart: Concerto No. 2, K.417; No. 3, K.447
___ MMO CD 3502 Baroque Brass And Beyond
___ MMO CD 3503 Music For Brass Ensemble

Choice selections for the French Horn, drawn from the very best solo literature for the instrument. The pieces are performed by the foremost virtuosi of our time, artists affiliated with the New York Philharmonic, Boston, Chicago, Cleveland and Philadelphia Orchestras. The Julliard School, Curtis Institute of Music, Indiana University, University of Toronto and Metropolitan Opera Orchestra.

Beginning	Intermediate	Advanced	Level
___ MMO CD 3511	Mason Jones, Philadelphia Orch.		B
___ MMO CD 3512	Myron Bloom, Cleveland Symphony		B
___ MMO CD 3513	Dale Clevenger, Chicago Symphony		I
___ MMO CD 3514	Mason Jones, Philadelphia Orch.		I
___ MMO CD 3515	Myron Bloom, Cleveland Symphony		A
___ MMO CD 3516	Dale Clevenger, Chicago Symphony		A
___ MMO CD 3517	Mason Jones, Philadelphia Orch.		I
___ MMO CD 3518	Myron Bloom, Cleveland Symphony		A
___ MMO CD 3519	Dale Clevenger, Chicago Symphony		I

The repertoire and editions used in the Laureate Series correspond to the approved music lists of various Music Education Associations and may be performed as contest solos in State Music Festivals. Contest regulations, such as time limitations have been taken into consideration.

Music Minus One CLARINET Compact Discs

___ MMO CD 3201 Mozart Clarinet Concerto in A major
___ MMO CD 3202 Weber Clarinet Concerto No. 1 in F minor, Op. 73
Stamitz Clarinet Concerto No. 3 in Bb major
___ MMO CD 3203 Spohr Clarinet Concerto No. 1 in C minor, Op. 26
___ MMO CD 3204 Weber Clarinet Concertino, Opus 26
___ MMO CD 3205 First Chair Clarinet Solos *Orchestral Excerpts*
___ MMO CD 3206 The Art Of The Solo Clarinet *Orchestral Excerpts*
___ MMO CD 3207 Mozart: Quintet for Clarinet and Strings in A, K.581
___ MMO CD 3208 Brahms: Sonatas Opus 120, Nos. 1 & 2
___ MMO CD 3209 Weber: Grand Duo Concertant - Wagner: Adagio
___ MMO CD 3210 Schumann Fantasy Pieces, Opus 73, Three Romances
___ MMO CD 3211 Easy Clarinet Solos, Student Editions 1-3 years
___ MMO CD 3212 Easy Clarinet Solos, Student Editions 1-3 years, vol. 2
___ MMO CD 3213 Easy Jazz Duets, Student Editions, 1-3 years

Choice selections for the Clarinet, drawn from the very best solo literature for the instrument. The pieces are performed by the foremost virtuosi of our time, artists affiliated with the New York Philharmonic, Boston, Chicago, Cleveland and Philadelphia Orchestras. The Julliard School, Curtis Institute of Music, Indiana University, University of Toronto and Metropolitan Opera Orchestra.

Beginning	Intermediate	Advanced	Level
___ MMO CD 3221	Jerome Bunke, Clinician		B
___ MMO CD 3222	Harold Wright, Boston Symphony		B
___ MMO CD 3223	Stanley Drucker, N.Y. Philharmonic		I
___ MMO CD 3224	Jerome Bunke, Clinician		I
___ MMO CD 3225	Stanley Drucker, N.Y. Philharmonic		A
___ MMO CD 3226	Harold Wright, Boston Symphony		A
___ MMO CD 3227	Stanley Drucker, N.Y. Philharmonic		I
___ MMO CD 3228	Stanley Drucker, N.Y. Philharmonic		I A
___ MMO CD 3229	Harold Wright, Boston Symphony		A

The repertoire and editions used in the Laureate Series correspond to the approved music lists of various Music Education Associations and may be performed as contest solos in State Music Festivals. Contest regulations, such as time limitations have been taken into consideration.

Music Minus One BROADWAY Shows

___ MMO CD 1016 LES MISERABLES/PHANTOM OF THE OPERA
___ MMO CD 1067 GUYS AND DOLLS
___ MMO CD 1100 WEST SIDE STORY   2 CD Set
___ MMO CD 1110 CABARET   2 CD Set
___ MMO CD 1130 ANDREW LLOYD WEBBER HITS
___ MMO CD 1151 JEKYLL & HYDE
___ MMO CD 1173 CAMELOT
___ MMO CD 1174 MY FAIR LADY   2 CD Set
___ MMO CD 1175 OKLAHOMA
___ MMO CD 1176 THE SOUND OF MUSIC   2 CD Set
___ MMO CD 1177 SOUTH PACIFIC
___ MMO CD 1178 THE KING AND I   2 CD Set
___ MMO CD 1179 THE FIDDLER ON THE ROOF 2 CD Set
___ MMO CD 1180 CAROUSEL
___ MMO CD 1181 PORGY AND BESS
___ MMO CD 1183 THE MUSIC MAN
___ MMO CD 1184 SHOWBOAT
___ MMO CD 1187 HELLO DOLLY   2 CD Set
___ MMO CD 1186 ANNIE GET YOUR GUN   2 CD Set
___ MMO CD 1189 OLIVER   2 CD Set
___ MMO CD 1193 SUNSET BOULEVARD
___ MMO CD 1197 SMOKEY JOE'S CAFE
___ MMO CD 1198 WALT DISNEY FAVORITE SONGS

Music Minus One ALTO SAX Compact Discs

___ MMO CD 4101 Easy Solos, Student Editions, Beginning Level vol. 1
___ MMO CD 4102 Easy Solos, Student Editions, Beginning Level vol. 2
___ MMO CD 4103 Easy Jazz Duets, Student Editions, 1-3 years
___ MMO CD 4104 For Saxes Only, Arr. by Bob Wilber

Choice selections for the Alto Sax, drawn from the very best solo literature for the instrument. The pieces are performed by the foremost virtuosi of our time, artists affiliated with the New York Philharmonic, Boston, Chicago, Cleveland and Philadelphia Orchestras. The Julliard School, Curtis Institute of Music, Indiana University, University of Toronto and Metropolitan Opera Orchestra.

Beginning	Intermediate	Advanced	Level
___ MMO CD 4111	Paul Brodie, Canadian Soloist		B
___ MMO CD 4112	Vincent Abato, Metropolitan Opera Orch.		B
___ MMO CD 4113	Paul Brodie, Canadian Soloist		I
___ MMO CD 4114	Vincent Abato, Metropolitan Opera Orch.		I
___ MMO CD 4115	Paul Brodie, Canadian Soloist, Clinician		A
___ MMO CD 4116	Vincent Abato, Metropolitan Opera Orch.		A
___ MMO CD 4117	Paul Brodie, Canadian Soloist, Clinician		A
___ MMO CD 4118	Vincent Abato, Metropolitan Opera Orch.		A

The repertoire and editions used in the Laureate Series correspond to the approved music lists of various Music Education Associations and may be performed as contest solos in State Music Festivals. Contest regulations, such as time limitations have been taken into consideration.

MMO MUSIC GROUP, INC., 50 Executive Boulevard, Elmsford, N.Y. 10523-1325

Music Minus One TENOR SAX Compact Discs

__ MMO CD 4201 Easy Tenor Sax Solos, Student Editions, 1-3 years
__ MMO CD 4202 Easy Tenor Sax Solos, Student Editions, 1-3 years
__ MMO CD 4203 Easy Jazz Duets with Rhythm Section, Beginning Level
__ MMO CD 4204 For Saxes Only, Arr. by Bob Wilber

Music Minus One TROMBONE Compact Discs

__ MMO CD 3901 Easy Solos, Student Editions, Beginning Level vol. 1
__ MMO CD 3902 Easy Solos, Student Editions, Beginning Level vol. 2
__ MMO CD 3903 Easy Jazz Duets, Student Editions, 1-3 years
__ MMO CD 3904 Baroque Brass & Beyond
__ MMO CD 3905 Music For Brass Ensemble

Choice selections for the Trombone, drawn from the very best solo literature for the instrument. The pieces are performed by the foremost virtuosi of our time, artists affiliated with the New York Philharmonic, Boston, Chicago, Cleveland and Philadelphia Orchestras. The Julliard School, Curtis Institute of Music, Indiana University, University of Toronto and Metropolitan Opera Orchestra.

Beginning	Intermediate	Advanced	Level
__ MMO CD 3911	Per Brevig, Metropolitan Opera Orch.		B
__ MMO CD 3912	Jay Friedman, Chicago Symphony		B
__ MMO CD 3913	Keith Brown, Soloist, Prof. Indiana Univ.		I
__ MMO CD 3914	Jay Friedman, Chicago Symphony		I
__ MMO CD 3915	Keith Brown, Soloist, Prof. Indiana Univ.		A
__ MMO CD 3916	Per Brevig, Metropolitan Opera Orch.		A
__ MMO CD 3917	Keith Brown, Soloist, Prof. Indiana Univ.		A
__ MMO CD 3918	Jay Friedman, Chicago Symphony		A
__ MMO CD 3919	Per Brevig, Metropolitan Opera Orch.		A

The repertoire and editions used in the Laureate Series correspond to the approved music lists of various Music Education Associations and may be performed as contest solos in State Music Festivals. Contest regulations, such as time limitations have been taken into consideration.

Music Minus One TRUMPET Compact Discs

__ MMO CD 3801 3 Trumpet Concerti Haydn/Telemann/Vivaldi
__ MMO CD 3802 Easy Solos, Student Edition, Beginning Level vol. 1
__ MMO CD 3803 Easy Solos, Student Edition, Beginning Level vol. 2
__ MMO CD 3804 Easy Jazz Duets with Rhythm Section, Beginning Level
__ MMO CD 3805 Music for Brass Ensemble
__ MMO CD 3806 First Chair Trumpet Solos
__ MMO CD 3807 The Art Of The Solo Trumpet
__ MMO CD 3808 Baroque Brass And Beyond
__ MMO CD 3809 The Arban Duets

Choice selections for the Trumpet, drawn from the very best solo literature for the instrument. The pieces are performed by the foremost virtuosi of our time, artists affiliated with the New York Philharmonic, Boston, Chicago, Cleveland and Philadelphia Orchestras. The Julliard School, Curtis Institute of Music, Indiana University, University of Toronto and Metropolitan Opera Orchestra.

Beginning	Intermediate	Advanced	Level
__ MMO CD 3811	Gerard Schwartz, N.Y. Philharmonic		B
__ MMO CD 3812	Armando Ghitalla, Boston Symphony		B
__ MMO CD 3813	Robert Nagel, Soloist, NY Brass Ensemble		I
__ MMO CD 3814	Gerard Schwartz, N.Y. Philharmonic		I
__ MMO CD 3815	Robert Nagel, Soloist NY Brass Ensemble		A
__ MMO CD 3816	Armando Ghitalla, Boston Symphony		I
__ MMO CD 3817	Gerard Schwartz, N.Y. Philharmonic		I
__ MMO CD 3818	Robert Nagel, Soloist, NY Brass Ensemble		A
__ MMO CD 3819	Armando Ghitalla, Boston Symphony		A
__ MMO CD 3820	Raymond Crisara, Concert Soloist		B
__ MMO CD 3821	Raymond Crisara, Concert Soloist		B
__ MMO CD 3822	Raymond Crisara, Concert Soloist		I

The repertoire and editions used in the Laureate Series correspond to the approved music lists of various Music Education Associations and may be performed as contest solos in State Music Festivals. Contest regulations, such as time limitations have been taken into consideration.

Music Minus One OBOE Compact Discs

__ MMO CD 3400 Albinoni Three Oboe Concerti Opus No. 3, No. 6, Opus 9 No. 2
__ MMO CD 3401 3 Oboe Concerti: Handel, Telemann, Vivaldi
__ MMO CD 3402 Mozart/Stamitz Oveo Quartets in F major (K.370; Op. 8 #3

Music Minus One DRUMMER Compact Discs

__ MMO CD 5001 MODERN JAZZ DRUMMING, 2 CD Set
__ MMO CD 5002 FOR DRUMMERS ONLY!
__ MMO CD 5003 WIPE-OUT!
__ MMO CD 5004 SIT IT!
__ * MMO CD 5005 DRUM STAR
__ * MMO CD 5006 DRUMPADSTICKSKIN
__ * MMO CD 5007 LIGHT MY FIRE
__ * MMO CD 5008 FIRE AND RAIN
__ * MMO CD 5009 CLASSICAL PERCUSSION, 2 CD Set
* Winter '95/Spring '96 Release

Music Minus One BANJO Compact Discs

__ MMO CD 4401 Bluegrass Banjo
__ MMO CD 4402 Play The Five String Banjo, vol. 1, Dick Weissman
__ MMO CD 4403 Five String Banjo, vol. 2, Dick Weissman

Music Minus One BASS VIOLIN Compact Discs

__ MMO CD 4301 Beginning & Intermediate Bass Solos
__ MMO CD 4302 Intermediate & Advanced Bass Solos

Music Minus One INSTRUMENT METHODS

__ MMO CD 7001 Rutgers University Music Dictation Series
6 CD Set   Deluxe Album $98.00
__ MMO CD 7002 The Music Teacher
__ MMO CD 7003 The Complete Guitar Method
__ MMO CD 7004 Evolution Of The Blues
__ MMO CD 7005 Art Of Improvisation, vol. 1
__ MMO CD 7006 Art Of Improvisation, vol. 2

MMO MUSIC GROUP, INC., 50 Executive Boulevard, Elmsford, N.Y. 10523-1325